# DEDICATION

*"We would not have historic sites like Evergreen Cemetery if it were not for Veronica Alease Davis."*

—Virginia Delegate Delores McQuinn

I am here to say we would not have those historic sites—
or the history they hold—if it were not for **John Coleman**,
the Hampton Police Officer whose bravery saved my life at the age of
four, when my life was nearly taken by a close relative at Bay Shore
Beach.

Because you stepped in on that day, I was given the gift of life.
I have spent it helping others and fighting to preserve
the places and stories that matter.

**Thank you for making that possible.**

# ACKNOWLEDGEMENTS

I want to extend my deepest thanks to the people who helped bring this book to life.

To my son, Cornell M. Burke — your light, laughter, and love for learning inspired every stroke of these pages. You remind me daily why our stories must be told.

To my uncle, John H. Davis, Jr., thank you for always believing in me and for passing down the value of history, heritage, and hard work.

I also wish to extend my sincere appreciation to Former First Lady Laura Bush, whose early support of my first book reminded me that stories rooted in truth and education have the power to reach hearts across every aisle. Your encouragement meant the world.

With profound gratitude, I recognize Former First Lady Michelle Obama and President Barack Obama for their support of my community efforts. Your recognition uplifted not just my work, but the people and places I serve. Thank you for seeing value in the stories we protect.

To my dear friend of over two decades, Rennie Marvel, thank you for your constant encouragement, creative insight, and unwavering belief in the power of this work. Your friendship has meant more than words can say.

To JoAnn Roberts, your strength and legacy are forever woven into the fabric of my life and this work.

To my paternal sisters and brothers and my Georgia family may you achieve the goals that you desire,

To the educators, parents, and caregivers who share this book with children — thank you for planting seeds of pride, knowledge, and identity.

And finally, to every child who opens these pages: May you see yourself reflected in history and feel empowered to shape the future.

# COLORING HISTORY:
# MAGGIE LENA WALKER
## FIRST FEMALE BANK PRESIDENT

Coloring History: Maggie Lena Walker First Female Bank President
Written and created by Veronica Alease Davis

First edition

Published by Davis Burke Enterprises
Published in the United States of America

Library of Congress Control Number: 2025919406
ISBN: 9798993098609 (paperback)

For educational and recreational use.
Recommended for ages 7-12 (Grades 2-6).

Publisher's Cataloging-in-Publication Data

Davis, Veronica Alease Davis
Coloring History: Maggie Lena Walker – First Female Bank President / Veronica Alease Davis. — First edition.

p. cm.

Summary: A documentary-style coloring and educational book for children and young adults introducing the life, leadership, and legacy of Maggie Lena Walker, the first African American woman to charter and serve as president of a bank in the United States. Includes bibliographical references.

Walker, Maggie L., 1864-1934 — Juvenile literature.
African American women bankers — Biography — Juvenile literature.
African American women — Biography — Juvenile literature.
Bankers — United States — Biography — Juvenile literature.
Coloring books — Juvenile literature.
I. Title: Maggie Lena Walker, first female bank president.

Dewey Decimal Classification: 332.1092 B
Library of Congress Classification: E185.97.W35

Series: Coloring History

Printed in the United States of America

# HOW TO USE THIS BOOK

Welcome to **Coloring History™!** This book invites you to explore the remarkable life of **Maggie Lena Walker**, the first African American woman to charter and serve as president of a bank in the United States. Her vision, leadership, and dedication to community empowerment continue to inspire people today.

Here's how to enjoy your journey through history:

## Read the Captions
Each coloring page shows an important moment in Maggie Lena Walker's life. Read the short sentence to learn what's happening.

## Color the Pictures
Use crayons or colored pencils—there's no wrong way to color! Add your own creativity to each page.

## Ask Questions
Talk with your teacher, parent, or friends about what you're learning. Why do you think Maggie Lena Walker's work made such a difference in her community?

## Use Your Imagination
Imagine what it was like to run a bank, publish a newspaper, or lead an organization that helped thousands of people. What kind of leader would you be?

## Keep Exploring
History is full of builders, dreamers, and leaders—just like you.

# TABLE OF CONTENTS

# PART I.
# EARLY LIFE & FAMILY

# "BORN IN RICHMOND, 1864"

Maggie Lena Walker was born in Richmond, Virginia, on July 15, 1864 — during the last days of the Civil War. Her mother, Elizabeth Draper, was once enslaved, and her father, Eccles Cuthbert, was an Irish American journalist. Maggie was born into a world of struggle and hope for freedom.

# ELIZABETH DRAPER: A MOTHER'S STRENGTH

Elizabeth Draper, Maggie's mother, was born enslaved in Virginia. She worked as a cook for Elizabeth Van Lew, a Union spy, and saw history unfold in the kitchen. Elizabeth taught Maggie the importance of education, dignity, and hard work — lessons that shaped Maggie's future.

# AN IRISH FATHER

Maggie's father, Eccles Cuthbert, was an Irish American journalist for the New York Herald. His relationship with Elizabeth Draper was brief, and he played no role in raising Maggie. Still, his presence in her family story added another layer to Maggie's identity in a divided world.

# WILLIAM MITCHELL, STEADY FATHER

After Maggie was born, her mother married William Mitchell, a butler at the Van Lew estate. William became a steady father figure, working as headwaiter at the Saint Charles Hotel. In their home on College Alley, Maggie learned lessons of hard work, pride, and self-respect.

# HOME ON COLLEGE ALLEY

The Mitchell family lived on College Alley, a small lane in Richmond near First African Baptist Church. Their home was simple but filled with love, faith, and hard work. Here, Maggie helped her mother and learned that true strength comes from family values, not wealth.

# FAITH AND FREEDOM

First African Baptist Church in Richmond was more than a place to pray. It was a center for education, activism, and community support. Young Maggie sat in its pews, hearing powerful sermons about freedom, dignity, and self-reliance — lessons she carried throughout her life.

19

# A FAMILY'S LOSS

When Maggie was twelve, her stepfather, William Mitchell, died. His death left the family without its main support. To survive, Maggie's mother took in laundry to earn money. This loss taught Maggie early about hardship, resilience, and the strength needed to carry on.

14

# WORKING BESIDE MOTHER

At twelve, Maggie helped her mother take in laundry after her stepfather's death. She carried heavy baskets through Richmond's streets, delivering clothes to wealthy families. These long days taught her responsibility, respect, and the importance of building dignity and opportunity for her own community.

16

# PART II:
# EDUCATION & EARLY LEADERSHIP

# LEARNING IN RICHMOND SCHOOLS

Maggie attended Richmond Public Schools soon after they opened to Black children. She loved learning and excelled in her studies, proving her talent and determination. For Maggie, every lesson was more than education — it was a step toward freedom and a brighter future.

Arithmetic

# JOINING
# THE INDEPENDENT ORDER OF ST. LUKE

At fourteen, Maggie joined the Independent Order of St. Luke, a group that helped African Americans through education, charity, and mutual aid. Here, she watched women lead and learned the power of teamwork, service, and community action — lessons that shaped her future.

19

# MT. OLYMPUS

Maggie Lena Walker attended Richmond Normal School with her close friend Wendell Dabney, who later founded a Cincinnati newspaper. Students affectionately called the school "Mt. Olympus." Among its notable alumni were John Mitchell, Jr., educator Marietta Chiles, and businesswoman Mary Burrell, shaping African American leadership for generations.

# GRADUATING WITH DIGNITY

In 1883, Maggie and her classmates refused to accept a segregated graduation. Instead of marching in the city's theater with divided seating, they held their own ceremony at school. Their protest showed courage and taught Maggie that dignity is worth more than approval.

# TEACHING AT VALLEY SCHOOL

After graduating in 1883, Maggie became a teacher at Valley School in Richmond. She taught discipline, self-respect, and hard work to her students, earning $35 a month to help her family. Teaching was her first calling, but it ended when she married in 1886.

## TEACHER BY DAY, BUSINESSWOMAN BY NIGHT

While teaching at Valley School, Maggie also worked part-time as an insurance agent with the Woman's Union, a group of Black women who supported their community. She studied accounting at night, learning that economic power was just as important to freedom as education.

# PART III:
# MARRIAGE & FAMILY

# MARRIAGE TO ARMSTEAD WALKER JR.

In 1886, Maggie married Armstead Walker Jr., a respected brick contractor in Richmond. Their marriage ended her teaching career but began a new chapter built on partnership and respect. Living in Jackson Ward, Maggie prepared to take on leadership in her community.

30

# BUILDING A HOUSEHOLD
## IN JACKSON WARD

After marrying, Maggie and Armstead settled in Jackson Ward, known as the "Harlem of the South." Their home reflected thrift and hard work, while the neighborhood showed the power of Black businesses and leaders. Living here inspired Maggie's dreams for her own community.

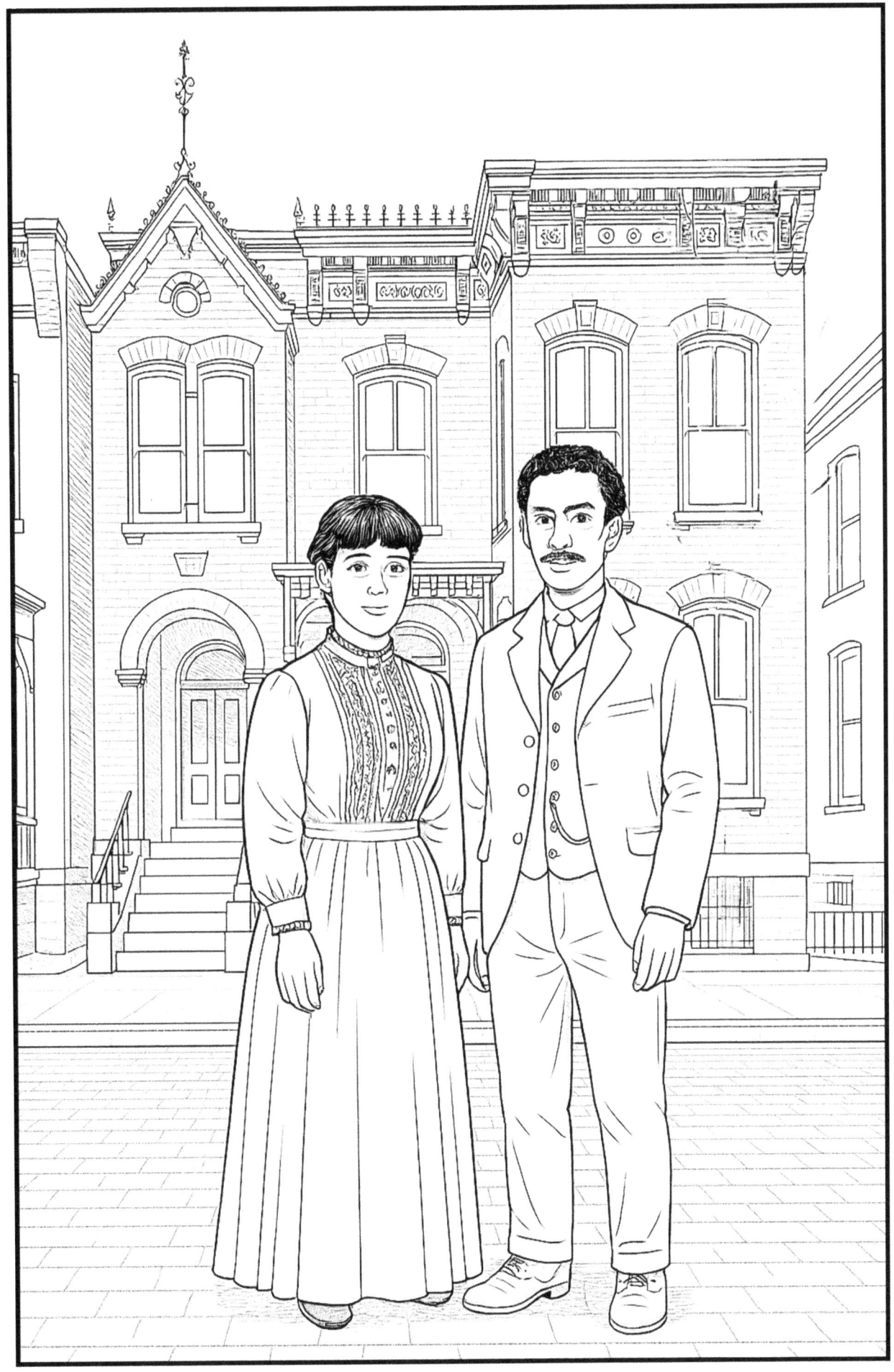

## LOSS OF A CHILD

In 1893, Maggie and Armstead welcomed a baby boy, but he lived only seven months. The loss brought deep sorrow to their family. Though rarely spoken of, this grief shaped Maggie's compassion for others and remained part of her family's story.

34

# THE WALKER FAMILY AT HOME

Maggie Lena Walker and her husband raised their two sons, Russell and Melvin, in this Richmond home. Their house was filled with love, learning, and community spirit. Maggie taught her children the values of hard work and leadership that would guide her lifelong mission to help others.

# ADOPTION OF POLLY ANDERSON

Maggie and Armstead opened their hearts and home to a young girl named Polly Anderson. Polly became like an older sister to the Walker boys, sharing in daily life and chores. For Maggie, adoption showed her belief that family is built on love, care, and commitment.

# HOSTING BLACK LEADERS IN THE WALKER HOME

Maggie and Armstead's home on East Leigh Street became a meeting place for Black leaders like W.E.B. Du Bois, Mary McLeod Bethune, and Langston Hughes. Around their table, they discussed education, civil rights, and the future. Maggie's hospitality helped inspire action and unity.

40

# PART IV:
# RISE IN THE
# INDEPENDENT ORDER OF ST. LUKE

# EARLY ROLES IN THE ORDER

While raising her family, Maggie stayed active in the Independent Order of St. Luke. She organized meetings, supported members, and encouraged women to lead. Known for her hard work and clear vision, Maggie prepared herself to guide the Order toward growth and lasting change.

43

# SAVING THE ORDER FROM COLLAPSE

By the late 1890s, the Independent Order of St. Luke was nearly bankrupt. In 1899, Maggie became its leader and quickly restored discipline, trust, and vision. She doubled membership in her first year and began turning the Order into a powerful force for progress.

# CREATING THE JUVENILE BRANCH

In 1895, Maggie Walker founded the Juvenile Branch of the Independent Order of St. Luke. The program taught children to save money, help neighbors, and take pride in their heritage. It prepared young people to become the next generation of leaders in their community.

# VISION FOR SOCIAL CHANGE

Maggie Walker believed freedom required more than laws — it needed economic power. Through the Order of St. Luke, she urged African Americans to save money, support Black businesses, and build their own institutions. She also championed women as leaders in business and community life.

# PART V:
# PUBLISHING & BANKING

# THE ST. LUKE HERALD

In 1902, Maggie Walker launched The St. Luke Herald, a newspaper for the Independent Order of St. Luke. As editor for over 30 years, she used it to share news, promote education, and inspire economic independence. The paper gave a powerful voice to the Black community.

50

# CHAMPIONING EDUCATION & EQUALITY

Through The St. Luke Herald, Maggie Walker promoted education and justice. She celebrated schools and student success while speaking out against Jim Crow laws and violence. For Maggie, learning and equality went hand in hand — both were keys to dignity and freedom.

52

# THE ST. LUKE PENNY SAVINGS BANK

In 1903, Maggie Walker made history by founding the St. Luke Penny Savings Bank. As the first Black woman to charter and lead a bank in the United States, she encouraged thrift, supported Black families and businesses, and proved that small savings could build great strength.

54

# THE BANK OPENS

On November 2, 1903, Maggie Walker opened the St. Luke Penny Savings Bank — the first bank led by a Black woman in the United States. Families, workers, and children brought their savings, building trust and pride. The bank gave dignity, hope, and financial power to the community.

TELLER

TELLER

SAFE
DERAIT
BOYKS
FOR FENT

56

# THE CHILDREN'S SAVINGS PROGRAM

Maggie Walker started a savings program for children at the St. Luke Penny Savings Bank. With pennies and nickels, young people opened accounts and learned thrift, dignity, and discipline. For many, it was their first time being welcomed as valued customers in a bank.

SAVINGS

58

# WOMEN LEADING IN FINANCE

Through the St. Luke Penny Savings Bank, Maggie Walker gave Black women leadership roles in finance. They worked as tellers, bookkeepers, and even board members, proving women could manage money and make decisions. Maggie showed the world that women belonged at the center of economic power.

# MERGING AND GROWING THE BANK

Maggie Walker led the St. Luke Penny Savings Bank through hard economic times. To protect families' savings, she encouraged mergers with other Black-owned banks, creating stronger institutions. By the 1920s, her efforts helped form Consolidated Bank and Trust, the largest Black-owned bank in the nation.

62

# PART VI:
# TRAGEDY & RESILIENCE

# THE LOSS OF ARMSTEAD WALKER

On June 20, 1915, tragedy struck when Maggie's husband, Armstead Walker, was accidentally killed at home. His sudden death left Maggie to carry on as both mother and leader. Through grief, she kept her family together and continued her work guiding the Order of St. Luke.

A black wreath is a traditional symbol of mourning, used to signify a death in the home
and express grief and sorrow, a practice dating back to the Victorian era.

# OVERCOMING HEALTH CHALLENGES

After a fall in the early 1900s and complications from diabetes, Maggie Walker began using a wheelchair. She installed an elevator in her home and adapted her Packard car for independence. From her wheelchair, she continued guiding the Order with strength and vision.

# ACTIVISM UNTIL THE END

Even while using a wheelchair, Maggie Walker remained a leader. She co-founded Richmond's NAACP, organized the Council of Colored Women, and supported boycotts against segregation. She also ran for public office and championed health care and schools, proving her courage and leadership never faded.

Maggie Lena Walker passed away on December 15, 1934, at age 70, after years of battling diabetes and complications from paralysis. Even in illness, she never stopped leading or serving her community. Her legacy lives on through the Order of St. Luke, the bank she founded, and the countless lives she inspired.

# FUN PAGES

# CHASE THE CHANGE!

Ms. Walker believed every penny had power—can **YOU** get the coins to the bank in time?

You have 5 minutes to find the correct path.

# ODD ONE OUT – MAGGIE L. WALKER

## INSTRUCTIONS:
### IN EACH ROW, CIRCLE THE ONE THAT DOES NOT BELONG.

1. MAGGIE'S LIFE AND WORK
FOUNDED ST. LUKE PENNY SAVINGS BANK
SERVED AS THE FIRST WOMAN BANK PRESIDENT IN THE U.S.
RAN FOR U.S. PRESIDENT IN 1928
EDITOR OF THE ST. LUKE HERALD NEWSPAPER

2. COMMUNITY LEADERSHIP
HELPED AFRICAN AMERICAN WOMEN GAIN EMPLOYMENT
SUPPORTED SCHOOLS AND EDUCATION
ORGANIZED THE INDEPENDENT ORDER OF ST. LUKE
INVENTED THE LIGHT BULB

3. PERSONAL LIFE
BORN IN RICHMOND, VIRGINIA
USED A WHEELCHAIR LATER IN LIFE
MOTHER WORKED AS A LAUNDRESS
BORN IN CHICAGO, ILLINOIS

4. LEGACY
HER HOME IS NOW A NATIONAL HISTORIC SITE
ADVOCATED FOR CIVIL RIGHTS
DIED IN 1934
WROTE THE GETTYSBURG ADDRESS

# COUNT ON CHANGE!

Count each coin, then graph it by coloring in the box every time you see it's picture.

| | | | | | | | | | |
|---|---|---|---|---|---|---|---|---|---|
| (penny) | | | | | | | | | |
| (nickel) | | | | | | | | | |
| (dime) | | | | | | | | | |
| (quarter) | | | | | | | | | |
| (dime) | | | | | | | | | |

73

# SAVE PENNIES, NICKELS AND DIMES WITH MS. WALKER

## WHAT IS THE TOTAL?

$ _____

73

# EXTRA! EXTRA!

# HELP MS. WALKER GET HOME FROM WORK!

# LEGACY OF LEADERSHIP

RICHMOND
SCHOOL
EDUCATION
STUDENTS
COMMUNITY
LEADERSHIP
SAVINGS
EQUALITY
ORDER
HERALD
BANK
FINANCE
SUFFRAGE
LIBRARY
WALKER
ERA
AGENT

```
L V E Q U A L I T Y
  E O D F I N A N C E
  A T U L I B R A R Y
  D E C W Z A     W R
  E S A V I N G S A D
  R C T L U K E B L N
S H I U K E R A K O
H O O R D E R T E M
I O N A G E N T R H
P L P V H Q N C M C
C O M M U N I T Y I
E E G A R F F U S R
```

HIDDEN WORD HINT: THE INDEPENDENT ORDER OF ST. _____

# ANSWER KEYS

# What Did You Learn About Maggie Lena Walker?

$

☆

☆   ☆                    ☆   ☆

# CHASE the CHANGE!

Ms. Walker believed every penny had power—can **YOU** get the coins to the bank in time?

You have 5 minutes to find the correct path.

78

# ODD ONE OUT
## MAGGIE L. WALKER

### INSTRUCTIONS:
IN EACH ROW, CIRCLE THE ONE THAT DOES NOT BELONG.

1. MAGGIE'S LIFE AND WORK
FOUNDED ST. LUKE PENNY SAVINGS BANK
SERVED AS THE FIRST WOMAN BANK PRESIDENT IN THE U.S.
RAN FOR U.S. PRESIDENT IN 1928
EDITOR OF THE ST. LUKE HERALD NEWSPAPER
(ODD ONE OUT → RAN FOR U.S. PRESIDENT IN 1928: SHE NEVER DID.)

2. COMMUNITY LEADERSHIP
HELPED AFRICAN AMERICAN WOMEN GAIN EMPLOYMENT
SUPPORTED SCHOOLS AND EDUCATION
ORGANIZED THE INDEPENDENT ORDER OF ST. LUKE
INVENTED THE LIGHT BULB
(ODD ONE OUT → INVENTED THE LIGHT BULB: THAT WAS THOMAS EDISON, NOT WALKER.)

3. PERSONAL LIFE
BORN IN RICHMOND, VIRGINIA
USED A WHEELCHAIR LATER IN LIFE
MOTHER WORKED AS A LAUNDRESS
BORN IN CHICAGO, ILLINOIS
(ODD ONE OUT → BORN IN CHICAGO, ILLINOIS: SHE WAS BORN IN RICHMOND.)

4. LEGACY
HER HOME IS NOW A NATIONAL HISTORIC SITE
ADVOCATED FOR CIVIL RIGHTS
DIED IN 1934
WROTE THE GETTYSBURG ADDRESS
(ODD ONE OUT → WROTE THE GETTYSBURG ADDRESS: THAT WAS ABRAHAM LINCOLN.)

# COUNT ON CHANGE!

Count each coin, then graph it by coloring in the box every time you see it's picture.

# SAVE PENNIES, NICKELS AND DIMES WITH MS. WALKER

## WHAT IS THE TOTAL?

$2.78

# EXTRA! EXTRA!

# HELP MS. WALKER
# GET HOME FROM WORK!

# LEGACY OF LEADERSHIP

RICHMOND
SCHOOL
EDUCATION
STUDENTS
COMMUNITY
LEADERSHIP
SAVINGS
EQUALITY
ORDER
HERALD
BANK
FINANCE
SUFFRAGE
LIBRARY
WALKER
ERA
AGENT

```
L  V  E  Q  U  A  L  I  T  Y
E  O  D  F  I  N  A  N  C  E
A  T  U  L  I  B  R  A  R  Y
D  E  C  W  Z  A  M  U  W  R
E  S  A  V  I  N  G  S  A  D
R  C  T  L  U  K  E  B  L  N
S  H  I  U  K  E  R  A  K  O
H  O  O  R  D  E  R  T  E  M
I  O  N  A  G  E  N  T  R  H
P  L  P  V  H  Q  N  C  M  C
C  O  M  M  U  N  I  T  Y  I
E  E  G  A  R  F  F  U  S  R
```

HIDDEN WORD HINT: THE INDEPENDENT ORDER OF ST. _____

# CREDITS & ACKNOWLEDGMENTS

This book was made possible through the dedicated research and preservation efforts of historians, archivists, and educators who have safeguarded the legacy of Maggie Lena Walker and the Independent Order of St. Luke.

## Archives & Institutions

Maggie L. Walker National Historic Site, National Park Service
Library of Virginia, Independent Order of St. Luke Records, 1935–1945
The Valentine, Richmond, Virginia

## Books

Marlowe, Woodruff Gertude. A Right Worthy Grand Mission: Maggie Lena Walker and the Quest for Black Economic Empowerment. Washington, D.C.: Howard University Press, 2003.

Davis, Veronica Alease. Inspiring African American Women of Virginia. Bloomington, IN: iUniverse, 2005.

## Scholarly Articles

Mayo, Anthony; Smith, Shandi Onise. "Maggie Lena Walker and the Independent Order of St. Luke." Harvard Business School, January 2017.

Lugar, Caleb W.; Garrett-Scott, Shennette; Novicevic, Milorad M.; Popoola, Ifeoluwa Tobi; Humphreys, John H.; Mills, Albert J. "The Historic Emergence of Intersectional Leadership: Maggie Lena Walker and the Independent Order of St. Luke." Leadership, Vol. 16, No. 2 (April 2020).

## Online Resources

"Independent Order of St. Luke: Maggie L. Walker National Historic Site." U.S. National Park Service.

"The St. Luke Herald." Maggie L. Walker National Historic Site, U.S. National Park Service.

Encyclopedia Virginia, "Maggie Lena Walker."

"Richmond Story: Lillian Payne and the Independent Order of St. Luke." The Valentine Museum.

## Games

Some design elements created using Canva Pro assets.

# VISIT THE MAGGIE L. WALKER NATIONAL HISTORIC SITE!

## DISCOVER AND LEARN ABOUT MAGGIE L. WALKER

The Maggie L. Walker National Historic Site (nps.gov/mawa) is a place in Richmond, Virginia to explore Maggie Walker's life and legacy. Learn how she became a pioneering businesswoman, community leader, and civil rights advocate.

# COMING SOON FROM COLORING HISTORY™

Celebrate the leaders who inspire us—from the classroom to the Oval Office and beyond. Join us on a journey through powerful legacies and vibrant stories designed for all ages to explore, color, and learn.

www.coloringhistorybooks.com

## Let's Stay Connected!

Join the movement to color history one page at a time.

**Follow Us Online:**

**Instagram & Pinterest:** @ColoringHistory

**Website**: www.coloringhistorybooks.com

## Shop Our Educational Resources

Explore exclusive coloring pages, lesson plans, and classroom materials.

**Find us on Teachers Pay Teachers**
**Search**: Veronica Davis
**Or visit**: TeachersPayTeachers.com/store/coloring-history-by-veronica-davis-educator

## Thank you for coloring history with us.